First Facts®

The Solar System

Revised
and
Updated

Neptune

by Ralph Winrich

Consultant:
Stephen J. Kortenkamp, PhD
Research Scientist
Planetary Science Institute, Tucson, Arizona

Capstone
press®

Mankato, Minnesota

First Facts is published by Capstone Press,
151 Good Counsel Drive, P.O. Box 669, Mankato, Minnesota 56002.
www.capstonepress.com

Library of Congress Cataloging-in-Publication Data
Winrich, Ralph.
    Neptune / by Ralph Winrich.—Rev. and updated.
    p. cm.—(First facts. The Solar system)
    Includes bibliographical references and index.
    ISBN-13: 978-1-4296-0726-1 (hardcover)
    ISBN-10: 1-4296-0726-2 (hardcover)
    1. Neptune (Planet)—Juvenile literature. I. Title. II. Series.
QB691.W56 2008
523.48'1—dc22   2007003534

Summary: Discusses the orbit, atmosphere, surface features, and exploration of Neptune.

Editorial Credits
Gillia Olson, editor; Juliette Peters, designer and illustrator; Jo Miller, photo researcher;
Scott Thoms, photo editor

Photo Credits
Astronomical Society of the Pacific/NASA, 14, 15
Corbis/Bettmann, 20 (right)
Digital Vision, 16–17
Getty Images/Hulton Archive, 20 (left)
NASA/JPL, 5
Photodisc, cover, 1, 4, planet images within illustrations and chart, 6–7, 10, 13, 19, 21
Photo Researchers Inc./Science Photo Library/NASA, 9
Space Images/NASA/STScl, 16 (inset)

1 2 3 4 5 6 12 11 10 09 08 07

Table of Contents

Voyager 2 and Neptune

Without a **telescope**, Neptune cannot be seen from Earth. With a telescope, Neptune looks like a tiny circle. People finally got a close-up view of the planet in 1989. The *Voyager 2* spacecraft flew by it and took pictures. Clouds swirl around this faraway planet.

Fast Facts about Neptune

Diameter: 30,760 miles (49,500 kilometers)
Average Distance from Sun: 2.8 billion miles (4.5 billion kilometers)
Average Temperature (cloud top): minus 279 degrees Fahrenheit (minus 173 degrees Celsius)
Length of Day: 16 hours, 7 minutes
Length of Year: 164 Earth years, 10 months
Moons: 13
Rings: 5 or 6

5

The Solar System

    Neptune is the eighth planet from the Sun. It is the smallest of the four giant planets. Jupiter, Saturn, and Uranus are the other giant planets.

    The rest of the planets are smaller than Neptune. Mercury, Venus, Earth, and Mars are the closest planets to the Sun.

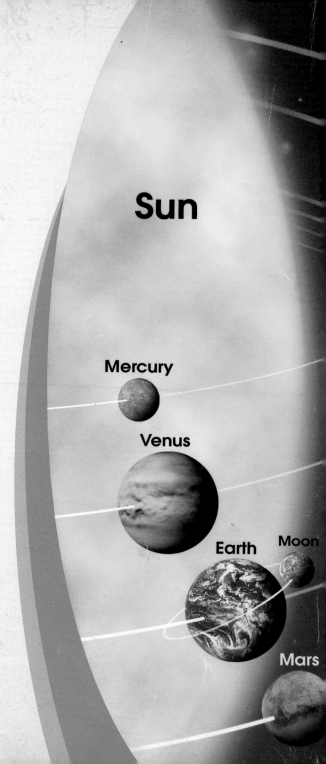

Sun

Mercury

Venus

Earth

Moon

Mars

Jupiter

Saturn

Uranus

Neptune

Neptune's Atmosphere

A planet's **atmosphere** is made up of the gases that surround it. Neptune's atmosphere is mostly hydrogen, helium, and methane. Methane gas makes the planet look blue.

Wispy, white clouds move quickly around Neptune's atmosphere. They cast shadows on the thick clouds below.

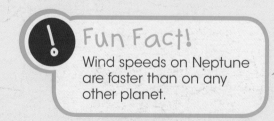

Fun Fact!
Wind speeds on Neptune are faster than on any other planet.

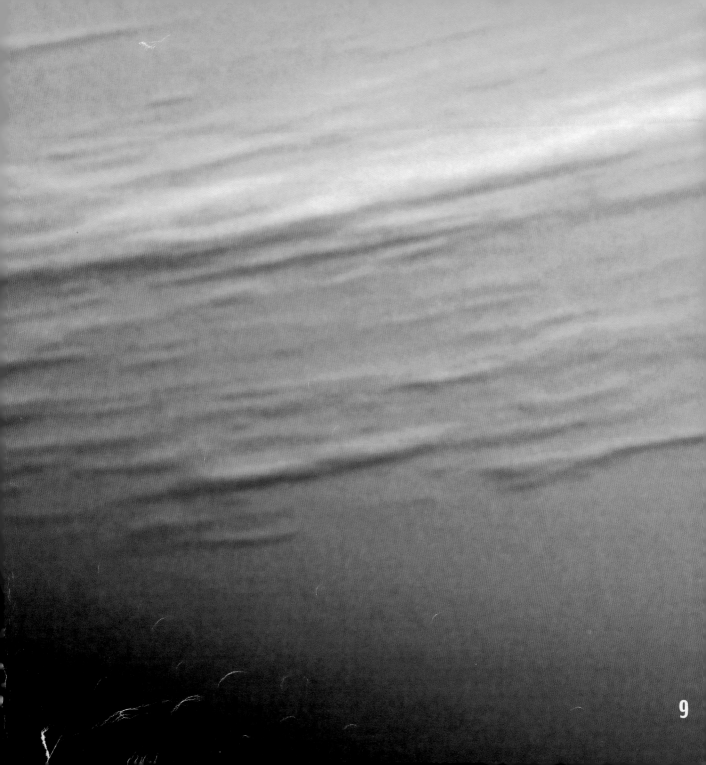

9

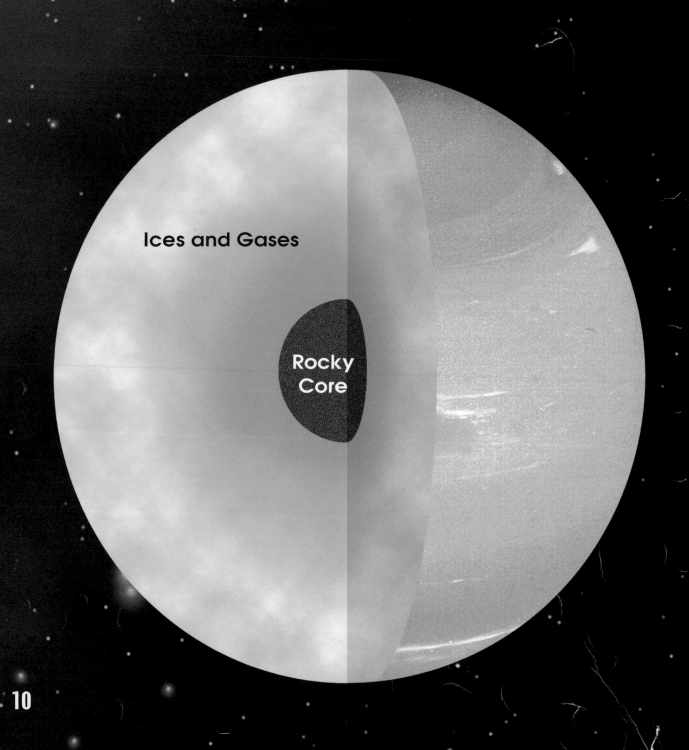

Neptune's Makeup

Neptune is mostly made up of ice and gas. Neptune's only solid part is its rocky **core**. The rest of the planet is a thick soupy mixture of ice and gas.

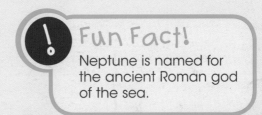

Fun Fact!

Neptune is named for the ancient Roman god of the sea.

How Neptune Moves

As Neptune circles the Sun, it spins on its **axis**. Neptune takes nearly 165 Earth years to circle the Sun. Neptune spins once in 16 hours, 7 minutes.

Neptune is the farthest planet from the Sun. Neptune's path around the Sun sometimes takes it farther away than the **dwarf planet** Pluto.

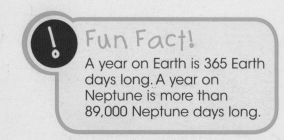

Fun Fact!

A year on Earth is 365 Earth days long. A year on Neptune is more than 89,000 Neptune days long.

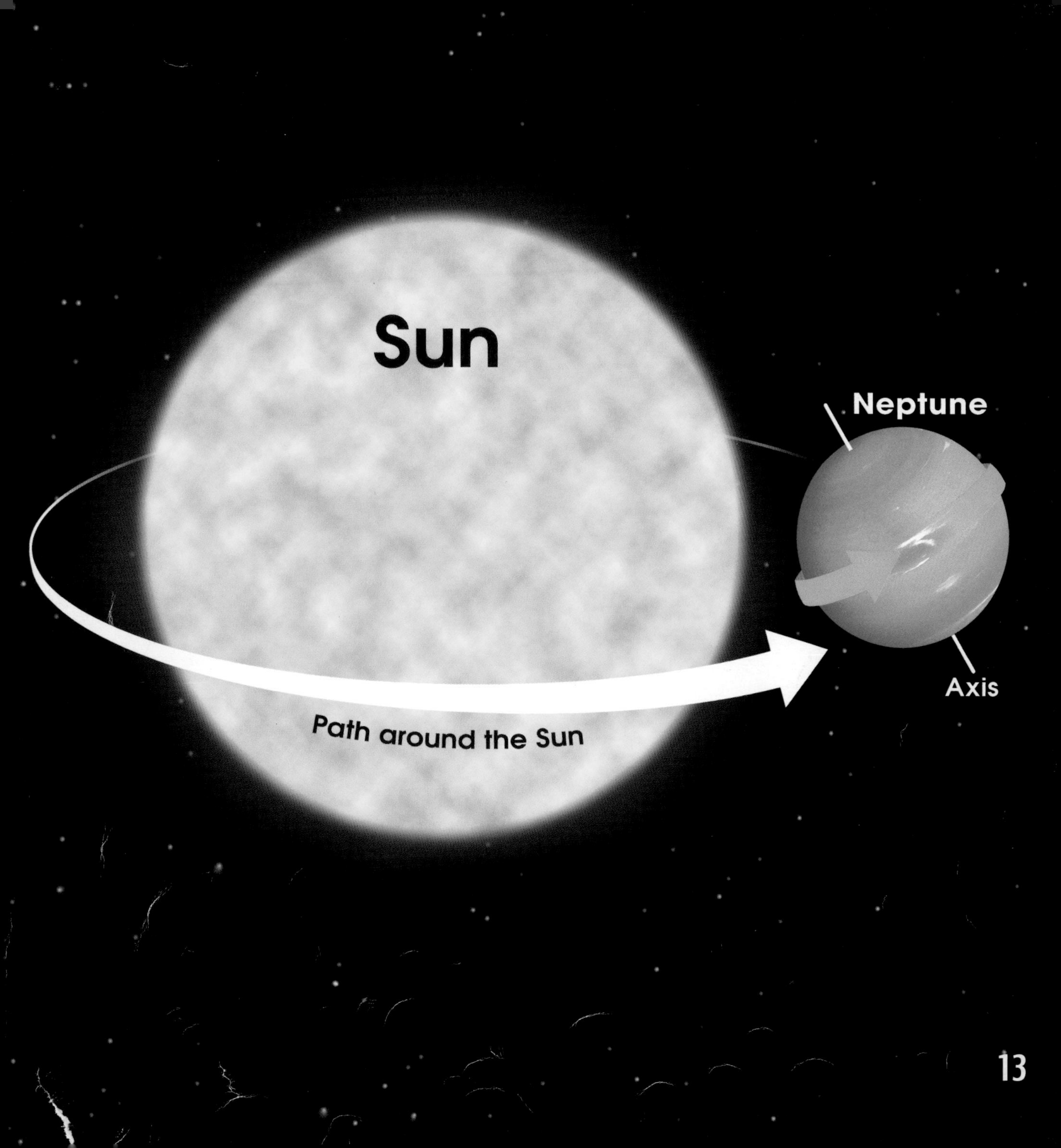

Sun

Neptune

Axis

Path around the Sun

geyser on Triton

Moons and Rings

Neptune has 13 moons. The largest moon is Triton. Triton has a thin atmosphere. It also has **geysers** that shoot out black clouds of gas and dust.

Neptune has faint rings made of dust. One ring seems to be only half there. Scientists aren't sure if Neptune has five rings or six rings.

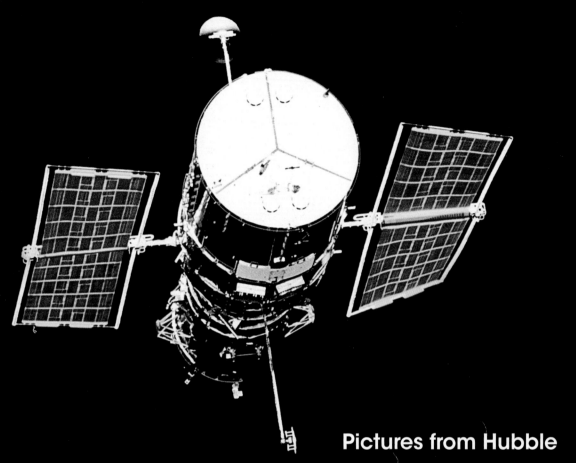

Pictures from Hubble

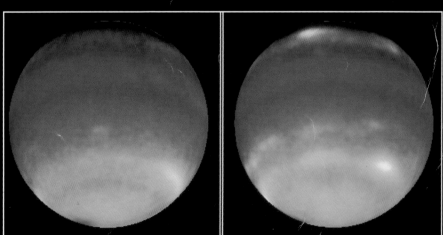

Studying Neptune

Scientists have no plans to send more spacecraft to Neptune. Today, scientists use telescopes to study the planet. The Hubble Space Telescope has shown new cloud features on Neptune.

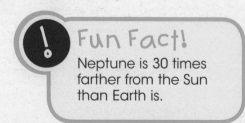

! **Fun Fact!**
Neptune is 30 times farther from the Sun than Earth is.

Comparing Neptune to Earth

Neptune and Earth are very different. Earth is a rocky planet. Neptune is a soupy mixture of gas and ice. Neptune's atmosphere is filled with gases that are **poisonous** to people. People can't live there. Instead, scientists will continue to study this strange world from afar.

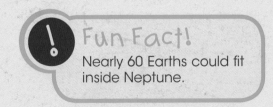

Fun Fact!
Nearly 60 Earths could fit inside Neptune.

Size Comparison

Neptune

Earth

Amazing but True!

The people who discovered Neptune didn't actually see it. In the 1840s, John Couch Adams and Urbain Le Verrier thought an unknown planet was affecting Uranus' movement. They used math to figure out where the new planet would be found. In 1846, other scientists used this information to spot Neptune with telescopes.

Adams

Le Verrier

Planet Comparison Chart

Planet	Size Rank (1=largest)	Makeup	1 Trip Around the Sun (Earth Time)
Mercury	8	rock	88 days
Venus	6	rock	225 days
Earth	5	rock	365 days, 6 hours
Mars	7	rock	687 days
Jupiter	1	gases and ice	11 years, 11 months
Saturn	2	gases and ice	29 years, 6 months
Uranus	3	gases and ice	84 years
Neptune	4	gases and ice	164 years, 10 months

Glossary

atmosphere (AT-muhss-feehr)—the layer of gases that surrounds some planets and moons

axis (AK-siss)—an imaginary line that runs through the middle of a planet or moon; a planet spins on its axis.

core (KOR)—the inner part of a planet that is made of metal or rock

dwarf planet (DWORF PLAN-it)—a round object that moves around the Sun, but is too small to be a planet

geyser (GYE-zur)—a hole in the ground where gas and dust shoot up in bursts

poisonous (POI-zuhn-uhss)—harmful if swallowed or breathed in

telescope (TEL-uh-skope)—an instrument that makes faraway objects appear larger and closer

Read More

Chrismer, Melanie. *Neptune.* Scholastic News Nonfiction Readers. New York: Children's Press, 2007.

Olien, Rebecca. *Exploring the Planets in Our Solar System.* Objects in the Sky. New York: PowerKids Press, 2007.

Orme, Helen, and David Orme. *Let's Explore Neptune.* Space Launch! Milwaukee: Gareth Stevens, 2007.

Internet Sites

FactHound offers a safe, fun way to find Internet sites related to this book. All of the sites on FactHound have been researched by our staff.

Here's how:
1. Visit *www.facthound.com*
2. Choose your grade level.
3. Type in this book ID **1429607262** for age-appropriate sites. You may also browse subjects by clicking on letters, or by clicking on pictures and words.
4. Click on the **Fetch It** button.

FactHound will fetch the best sites for you!

Index